HARRY POTTER JOKE KIDS

The Unofficial Book of Funny Laugh-out-Loud Harry Potter Jokes and One-Liners

Written by: Nina Riddle

Harry Potter Jokes for Kids: The Unofficial Book of Funny Laugh-out-Loud Harry Potter Jokes and One-Liners

HARRY POTTER JOKES FOR KIDS

How do turn a donkey into a unicorn? With a horserer's stone.

Why didn't the ant get into Hogwarts? She was a Buggle.

Where do Death Eaters go on vacation when they want to get a sun tan? Hexico City.

What do you call a flattened dragon? A lizard trading card.

Where do older wizards go when they want to listen to swing music with a fun rhythm? Jazzkaban.

What is Cho Chang's favourite salad? Ravenslaw.

What is the worst thing you can wear on your feet? A You-Know-Shoe.

What's another word for a poorly-constructed overpass? A dumbridge.

Who is Sir Patrick Nolegs? Leader of the Headless Runts.

What do call a paid informant in Azkaban? A golden snitch.

How do pigs choose which wizards to be friends with? With the Snorting Hat.

What's the fastest way to get to the bathroom? Loo powder.

What was the name of the nosy witch journalist who only did food stories? Pita Eater.

How does Cho Chang get to Hogwarts? She takes the cho cho train.

Which Ravenclaw ghost is always serving tea? The Tray Lady.

Which class at Hogwarts teaches you how to style a hippogriff? Hair of Magical Creatures.

What do you call a friendly wizard who spends a lot of time at the gym? A huffletuff.

Who cleans the merpeople's castle? Mermaids.

What is the name of the sleepy house-elf who lives at Hogwarts? Blinky.

What do call a witch who eats a lot of seafood? Tuna Lovefood.

What does Hagrid call his Great Dane when it's sleeping? A snorehound.

What book should you read if there isn't any food in the fridge? Fantastic Feasts and Where to Find Them.

What does Professor Fingers teach? Handsmogrification.

Which teacher at Hogwarts has never been in love? Professor Rockheart.

Which painting will get you in a lot of trouble if you hang on a wall? He-Who-Must-Not-Be-Framed.

What is the name of the English wizarding school for orchestra conductors? Nicebaton.

Which magical creature is black and fluffy and will sniff out a buried car? A Miffler.

How many stars out of 10 did the Academy give the Harry Potter movies? Nine and three quarters.

What do vampires call a human who doesn't taste very good? Dudblood.

Which magical creature loves to do landscaping? Mowtruckles.

How do toads hide from predators? With an invisibility croak.

What do dentists cast on teeth when they find a cavity? The Filling Curse.

Which portrait guards the entrance to the Gryffindor hair salon? The Hat Lady.

Where can you buy a magical ruler and protractor set? Diagonal Alley.

Which potion will make you look like Santa Clause? The hollyjuice potion.

Why did the werewolf live in a barn? His name was Fenrir Hayback.

What do you call a wizard friend who loans you money? A palleon.

What do call a wizard with stinky shoes? A Death Feeter.

Where do African wizards go to recover when they've played too much music? St. Bongo's Hospital of Magical Maladies and Injuries.

What spell will shoo away a barking dog? Expelliarmutt.

What do shape shifters hang on their walls? Bog art.

What do you call a wheel that explodes with a flash of colored light? Wizarding tireworks.

What you call a magical barrier that protects you from evil? Da fence against the dark arts.

Who do you need to get permission from if you want to perform a sad play? The Ministry of Tragic.

Why does a professor with the huge nose teach? Defense Against the Dark Farts.

When wizards go fishing what do they use as bait? Bobberworms.

What do you call a secret society of tollbooth operators? The Order of the Feenix.

Where do you catch the train to bring you back to London? Platform Nine and Three Sickles.

How do giant hawks flavor their pasta sauce? Oregano and basilisk.

Where do androids keep their safety deposit box? Gringbotts.

What do you call a chaser who never scores a point? An eraser.

What do call a creature that's half horse, half eagle, and upset at something you just said? Hippomiffed.

What spell creates enough water for everyone? Aguaplenty.

Why did Amelia Bones order a crate of lobsters? She was made the head of the Department Magical Claw Enforcement.

What do you call a scruffy-looking fellow who designs funeral urns? A hairy potter.

What spell will fix an injured bird? Reparrot.

What do you call the people who clean up after a Quidditch game? Neaters.

What do call a wand that sprays glue on the walls? A roomstick.

What spell will harvest a grape vine in two seconds flat? Severus Grape.

What do you call a ghost who turns grapes into wine? A fermentor.

Where do princes and princesses hang out when they visit Hogsmeade? The Frog's Head.

How do you walk through a burned down building without getting hurt? With a Rubble-Head Charm.

Why do wizard doctors only use Knuts and Galleons? They don't like Sickles.

What house did the zombie belong to? Whitherin.

Where do you practice filling up your car with gasoline? At the Fueling Club.

What do you call a bull who always keeps his word? An unbreakable cow.

What do you call a Quidditch player who spends a lot of time making potions? A beaker.

How do turn a rooster into a sheep? With a Farm Charm.

What do all witches carry in their purse to help them paint their nails? Toe-glass.

Which wizard village can sometimes be very hard to find? Fogsmeade.

What do call a squad of one-handed wizard safecrackers? The Unlocking Arm.

How do you counteract the Blaming Solution? With a Deflecting Draught.

Why was the Nimbus 1999 dumped by the Nimbus 2000? He was outdated.

What do you call a magical glass ball that fills with smokey images of great battles? A rememberbrawl.

What do you call someone that is half man, half horse, and has a big nose? A scentaur.

What do call a gang of wizard marbles? Mobstones.

What cleaning tool will appear only when the seeker truly needs it? The Broom of Requirement.

What spell will make someone run faster?
The Ranishing Charm.

How do you get a pair of binoculars to bake
you a cake? With Ocularmancy.

How do you find Hermione when she's
studying? Open all the gryffindoors and look
inside the broom closet.

Who is in charge of putting out small fires in
a wizard's home? The douse-elf.

Who keeps track of all the important wizards and witches who attended Hogwarts? The famekeeper.

What do type of music do swamp creatures listen to? Hinkyfunk.

What do you call a tree that makes loud noises when it walks around at night? A clomping willow.

What street can you find shops that sell things related to the Dark Arts of Bricklaying? Blockturn Alley.

Why do mimes make good alchemists? They're good with motions.

What wizarding sweets do cheerleaders buy at Honeydukes? Exploding Pompoms.

What do you call a doctor who can cure a werewolf bite? A cure-blood.

What was the name of the most famous German wizard? Berlin.

What was the name of the Hufflepuff ghost who used to be a vampire hunter? Bat Fryer.

How can you see the future with only some tea leaves and a television screen? With Tivination.

What newspaper do the goblins read at Gringotts? The Daily Profit.

What was the vampire's favorite portrait? The Bat Lady.

What did Professor McGonagall say about the Christmas present Dolores Umbridge gave her? It was an Ungiftable Purse.

What do you call someone who isn't very good at scoring points at Quidditch? A waffler.

What was the name of Dumbledore's pet fox? Phoenix.

Where do bullfrogs go to learn magic? Bogwarts.

What spell do farmers cast on their crops to deflect minor curses and insects? The Yield Charm.

How do get rid of annoying person with long pants? The smelly-legs Jinx.

How do you catch a wizard on a firebolt broomstick? With a firebolt extinguisher.

What do you call a yellow stick used to cast spells? A blonde wand.

What do call a small creature with a head like a bald potato that's been turned to stone? A harden gnome.

Which potion will make you grow six inches? The tallyjuice potion.

What do wizards eat when they go to the beach? Sandwitches.

What do call an ugly wolf that lives in your attic? A ghoooooooooooool.

Which professor teaches you how to look after a three-headed dog? Professor Pooch.

What do you call rug that protects you from dementor? A matronus.

How do dogs protects themselves from tigers? Catsbane.

How do you play Dynamite Quidditch? With a boomstick.

What book did Carsandra Vanblatsky write?
Unfogging the Window, a guide to basic
fortune-telling methods.

What's a squirrel's favorite drink?
Nutterbeer.

Where can you buy Peppermint Toads?
Follow the peppermint road!

How do get kids to eat more lettuce? Serve
them Every Flavor Greens.

Which Slytherin ghost has unpredictable temper tantrums? The Moody Baron.

What is Vincent Crabbe's favourite food? Vincent Lobbster.

What do the Malfoys serve for dessert? Jelly Smugs.

What award from Witch Weekly does Hermione want to win? The Most-Charming File award.

What does Professor Sinistart teach?
Gastronomy.

What was the name of Horace Slughorn's
hand-picked club of mediocre witches and
wizards? The Shrug Club.

What type of biscuits will turn you into a
screeching bird? Canary Screams.

What do you call an old leprechaun's walking
cane? A pixie stick.

Which organization regulates the rules for magical card games? The Ministry of Magic the Gathering.

Where do goblins buy their candy? Moneydukes.

What do you call an owl that buries letters instead of delivering them? Digwidgeon.

What was the name of the goblin who worked at the library? Gripbook.

What do you call follower of Voldemort who copies your homework? A Death Cheater.

What does a mouse keeper guard? The moleposts.

What do you call a pet rat that likes to play word games? Scrabbler.

Where do comets get permission to fly through the sky? At Ministry of Meteorological Transportation.

What is a Norwegian Ridgeback's favourite dessert? Sherbert.

Which wizarding magazine focuses on how to make the world a better place? Transfiguration Tomorrow.

What is the name of the Hogwarts poltergeist who will bring you tea and biscuits? Jeeves.

How does a wizard say he forgot his money? "I don't got knuttin."

What's the name of the shop that sells pants to skeletons? Levi's Corpus.

What type dragon is always offering people cold drinks? The Norwegian Fridgeback.

What do you call someone who can't use magic but is very affectionate about wizards and witches? A Huggle.

Where can you buy a map of the wizarding world? Madam Malkin's Globes for all Occasions.

Why wasn't Fred invited to the beach? Last time he brought some Whizzing Fizzbees.

What is the name of the magical law enforcement softball team? The Mitt Wizards.

What day do Christmas decorations celebrate? Wreathday, the day they were first hung up.

What do call someone who speaks softly and wears spectacles? Mumbledore.

Why did dad turn mom into a gopher? She called him an acid pop.

Which monster likes to skateboard? Rampires.

What do you get when you charm a cow with a chocolate bar? Chocolate Bullfrogs.

What do call a witch who can turn herself into a giant butt? A fannymagus.

What do ducks bring to Christmas parties? Wizarding Quackers.

How do birds fix a broken bone? With a skele-crow potion.

Which house did the peacock join? Rufflepuff.

Who can fix a sailboat with a single potion? The Potions mast-er.

What does the house with the least amount of points get at the end of the year? The Mouse Cup.

Where can you buy a magic pie to throw in someone's face? Gambol and Crepes.

How are contenders chosen for the Triclown Tournament? With the Goblet of Fireworks.

What's the name of the vehicle that transports wizards and witches to emergency Halloween parties? The Fright Bus.

What spell has no effect on Dudley?
Wheezing Charm.

Which animal do you never want to be pen pals with? The howler monkey.

What type of broomstick flies so fast it makes you sick? The Vomit.

Where's a great place to hide your car? In the Ford-hidden Forest.

What do you call an hourglass that's not very good at telling time or making toast? A time-burner.

What did Hedwig name her doll? Wighead.

What was the name of Dudley's long lost handsome cousin? Studley.

What do you call a ginger bowlegged cat that got his hand bitten off by an alligator? Hookshanks.

What candy will become coated with iron oxide if left out in the rain too long? Cockroach Rusters.

What was the name of Neville's pet toad that won the chess tournament? Clevor.

What was the name of the house-elf who couldn't stop stealing things? Robby.

How do you get a cow as a patronus? With a Summoning Farm.

How much can you sell a horcrux for? 50 horbucks.

What do you call a Slytherin who doesn't get any birthday presents? Draco Notoy.

Where did Vernon Dursley work when he sold bob sleds? Cool Grunnings.

Where does the train leave for dental school? King's Floss Station.

Made in the USA
Lexington, KY
31 January 2018